Eldo

Psalms

for

Teens

CONCORDIA®

Copyright © 1992 Concordia Publishing House
3558 S. Jefferson Avenue, St. Louis, MO 63118-3968
Manufactured in the United States of America

Library of Congress Cataloging-in-Publication Data

Weisheit, Eldon.
     Psalms for teens / Eldon Weisheit.
        p.   cm.
     Based on the Good News Bible, the Bible in Today's English Version.
     Includes a topical index.
     Summary: Presents the message of Psalms 1–75 in contemporary language that addresses the situations and concerns of today's young people.
     ISBN 0-570-04599-1
     1. Bible. O.T. Psalms—Paraphrases, English. [1. Bible. O.T. Psalms—Paraphrases. 2. Prayer books and devotions. 3. Christian life.] I. Title.
BS1440.W43 1992
242'.63—dc20   92-33385

---

1 2 3 4 5 6 7 8 9 10   01 00 99 98 97 96 95 94 93 92

Dedicated to

the kids in the confirmation classes
of Fountain of Life Lutheran Church, Tucson, Arizona
from 1978 through 1993
(and those who are yet to come).
Thanks for letting me see God
in your lives.

Introduction

Teenager, these psalms are for you. But there's something I have to explain: The psalms in this book are not the psalms of the Bible. But I did study them—a lot—to see what their authors (often King David) were feeling when they wrote. I tried to feel what they felt, both in the situation in their lives and in their relationship with God. Then, as I wrote this book, I kept one eye on the biblical psalms and one eye on you.

The psalms are different from the other books of the Bible. Much of the Bible is history, the stories you learned in Sunday school. (If not, get with it.) The stories show that God is a part of human history. He made the world and stuck with it. He is part of the conversations in the Bible. He is one of the actors— that is, one who causes the action to happen. In fact, God was so eager to have a leading role in world history that He applied for citizenship and became a human being in Jesus Christ. The stories about Jesus show us what God says and does when He lives with us.

Part of the Bible gives us theology—that is, knowledge of God. The Old Testament prophets spoke and wrote the message of God for the people. The New Testament evangelists wrote letters that explain how God's action applies to the everyday lives of people. The theology of the Bible is not a vague feeling or a human philosophy; it says that God is real and we can depend on Him. Scripture recognizes all the problems and joys, strengths and weakness of people and tells us that God knows what is going on and that He is here to help.

Though the psalms contain both history and theology, they look at a situation from a different point of view. Psalms, by definition, are sacred songs and poems for the praise of God: worship. When God's people know His track record (that's history) and the way He thinks (that's theology), they want to rejoice

5

with Him (that's worship). The biblical psalms are great worship aids, because they show us that those who wrote them had learned well their lessons about God.

The psalms reveal also the feelings of their authors. The Psalter (the book of Psalms) contains a catalog of human feelings—expressions of joy and sadness, trust and doubt, fear and faith, despair and hope, loneliness and security. At times, some of the psalm writers seem to be paranoid. At other times, they show a faith that is on a solid rock.

These people were not afraid to reveal their emotions, because they knew God. When they were happy, they praised God. When they were scared, they blamed God. When they were angry at God, they told Him so. Some readers have been shocked to see that, at times, a writer of a psalm may have doubted God's presence or even asked Him to do wrong things. But that's the point. When the psalmists had feelings that caused them problems, they told God—and He helped them. The psalms are God's success stories. They were written by the people who heard Him and knew they could talk to Him about anything.

As I said, I wrote my psalms in this book with one eye on the Bible and the other on you. If the psalm writer talked about his king and nation, I thought about your governmental leaders and country. If he talked about going to the temple, I thought about your place in church. If he told God what made him happy or sad, angry or afraid, I thought about the things that might cause you to feel the same way.

As I wrote, I did not try to pretend that I was a teenager. I am a parish pastor and work with many people of all ages. However, I especially enjoy (and am worn out by) confirmation classes. I think I can recognize and identify with your life experiences just as I can with the people who wrote the biblical psalms.

My purpose in this book is to bring their and your experiences together. I hope that this process will help you express your feelings (all of them) to God. Think about what you have learned about God (history and theology), and use those things in your worship life. Your application may be very different from mine; that's fine. You might even like to write your own psalms. (It's fun.) I also hope that, as you read my psalms, you will go back and read the ones in the Bible. After all, it's God's Word that prompts us to worship Him. I pray that my words will encourage you to do exactly that.

Eldon Weisheit
Tucson, Arizona

Psalm 1

You will have more fun
    if you don't listen to those
        who tell you to do wrong things,
    if you don't follow those
        who lead you to dangerous places,
    if you don't go along with those
        who do not love God.
You will be better off if you listen to God,
    hear the stories about Jesus,
    and praise God in your heart.
Then you will be like a tree
    that grows tall and straight.
You will be able to do many things well.

But those who don't know God,
    who do not hear His Word and
    learn how to do what is right,
    they are like weeds
    that make a mess
    and must be pulled up
    and thrown away.

God wants to lead you
    because He knows
    where it is best for you to go.

Psalm 2

Why do parents yell at me?
Why do teachers assign things that I can't do?
Bullies laugh at me
    and call me bad names.
They say that I'm stupid
    because I go to church.
They even say bad things about Jesus.

But Jesus is with me.
He laughs with me,
    not at me.
He tells me that others can't hurt me
    because He loves me
    and is with me.
"I will tell those people
    that you are My friend," Jesus says.
I am glad that He takes care of me.

Psalm 3

A lot of people are mad at me.
They talk about me behind my back.
To my face they say
 that You won't help me.

But that's not true, is it, God?
You have helped me before.
I know it.
I'm scared now.
But I've been scared before,
 and You helped me.
So I'm asking You to help again.
I know You will.

I'm ready to go to sleep now.
I'm not going to worry anymore
 because I asked You to help.

Come on, God!
You can do it!

Psalm 4

Please listen to me, God.
A long time ago, when I was a little kid,
    when I was lost in the shopping center,
    I prayed, and You heard me.
Be kind to me now and
    and hear my prayer.

How long will people make fun of me?
How long will I feel ugly?
How long will I feel stupid?

I know You picked me to be Your friend.
I know You love me and help me.
But I want them to like me, too.
Help me like them,
    so they can like me.

Then when I go to sleep,
    I can feel good.
God, You're the only one
    who can help me.

Psalm 5

Please listen to me, God.
I have to talk to You.
I need someone to help,
    and You're the only one who can.

It's time for me to get out of bed.
I want You to be with me today.
I've got to know
    that You know I'm here.

You aren't happy when I do bad things.
I know that.
You don't like lies and angry words.
I know that.

But I also know that You love me.
You want me to talk to You.
You want us to be together.

And that's my problem, God.
Some of my friends don't know You.
And some don't like You.
When I am with them,
    I may forget You, too.

So please hear me now, God.
Love me so much
    that I will remember You all day.

Psalm 6

God, don't be mad at me!
Please don't punish me.
I know I do bad things.
But I still need You
    to be on my side.
I'm waiting for You to help me.

I cried last night
    before I went to sleep.
I wanted to cry at school today,
    but I drew pictures
        in my book instead,
    and I pushed the other kids
        in the lunch line.

Can You hear my crying, God,
    even when I'm not crying?
Please help me now!

Psalm 7a (vv. 1–9)

God, I need You!
Please hide me!
Protect me from those who find fault with me.
They want to make me feel bad about myself.
They want me to think that I am no good.

God, if I have done wrong,
    I need Your help.
Was I wrong when I told my parents what I thought,
    even though I knew they wouldn't like it?
Am I bad because I think about sex?
Am I no good because sometimes
    I don't want to go to church?

You have to help me, Lord!
Those at school who don't know You
    say I'm bad because I don't do what they want.
Those at church who say they know everything about You
    say I'm bad because I don't do what they want.
How do I know, Lord?
You are the only judge that counts, Lord.
You are the only one who can judge with
    innocent eyes and a holy heart.
You judge by what You see in my heart,
    not by what others say,
    and not even by what I say.

I don't always know what is right
    and what is wrong.
I know many who want to tell me,
    but I need someone who shows me.

And that's You, Jesus—only You.
You're the only one who forgives me
    when I am wrong.
Therefore I'll let You judge me.

Psalm 7b (vv. 10–17)

God, You are my bodyguard.
You're the one who makes me feel safe,
    even when I am in dangerous company.
People do lots of bad things all the time.
You already know that, Lord;
    so it's not that I am telling on them.
But I don't have to be afraid
    because there is evil in the world
    because You're here, too.

I was taught that original sin meant that
    sin came as standard equipment on us all.
But I think some people try to find new ways to sin.
They want to claim originality for their evil.
But You know them, Lord,
    just as You know me.
I'm not afraid of their evil,
    because You will take care of it.
I like Your justice, God,
    because it comes wrapped in mercy.

Psalm 8

God, You are the best!
You are so great
    that You don't need famous people
    to say how great You are.
Even a little baby can do it.

I like to look at all the beautiful things
    that You have made:
        the moon and the stars,
        the trees and the flowers,
        the birds and the bugs.

The other things You made
    don't give You any trouble.
But I do.
    (And other people do too.)
Why do You still like us people, God?
You have given us so much.
And we can do so many fun things.

I like the way You run this world, God!

Psalm 9

I want to tell everyone
    what You have done, God.
You make me so happy
    that I want to tell everyone.

The bullies are afraid to pick on me
    because You are my friend.
You are always fair,
    and You keep them from hurting me.

You're good to other people, too.
    Sometimes I want to be the bully,
        but You won't let me.

You love the new kid in class
    who acts like a nerd to get attention.
You care about the one
    who can't play ball
        and made our team lose.
You never forget anyone.

Thanks for taking good care of us.
And, oh yes:
Please take good care of Yourself, too;
    because without You, we're in big trouble.

Psalm 10

Why do You hide from me, God?
Why is it
    that when I need You the most,
    You seem the least available?

Do You know what people get away with around here?
Can't You see what is going on?
I've no complaints
    about how You take care of me.
I appreciate my home, country, school,
    food, health, and all that stuff.
Thank You for those gifts—
    and I mean it!

But how about those other people?
You take care of them
    just as well as You take care of me.
And look what they do, Lord.
Look!
I don't mean just the ones who smoke pot
    and drink beer in the parking lot.
I don't mean just those who steal
    and go to porno shops.
I don't mean just those who have sex with anyone
    and then have abortions.
I mean everyone, God!

Can't You see it?
Those who do the awful things brag about their sins.
Those who think they are better than others
    also brag about that.

20

Even the good ones are proud.
They want people to see their clothes and grades.
They want to tell about their trips and cars.
They laugh at poor people.
They hate people who are different.

It scares me, Lord,
    because I don't see anyone who is good.
But I do see You, Lord.
I know You love us all.
Please help me help others,
    but help me never hurt others.
Please help others help me,
    but help them never hurt me.

We all need Your help, Lord.

Psalm 11

I know that God knows—
    He knows what I say and what I do.
    He knows what I think and what I feel.
    Yet He loves me.
I feel safe with Him.

Don't tell me,
    "Come on, no one will know."
    No one can hide from God.

God doesn't live in a church building
    or up on a mountain.
His temple is all that He created.
He doesn't just wave to us
    or leave us messages on paper.
He was born as a baby named Jesus,
    who had a family, a church, a school
    like we do.
God is with us.
Whether we do good or bad,
    it makes no difference;
    He is here.

Some people are afraid of God.
They think He will find out about them.
But I am not afraid,
    because I know
    He already knows.

Psalm 12

Please help me, God!
I can't trust anyone but You.

All the kids are bad.
  They cheat at school.
  They lie all the time.
  They pretend they like each other,
    but they don't.

Make them shut up, God.
Don't let them say,
  "I'll do what I want!"
  "I'll say what I want!"
  "You can't stop me!"

And God said to me:
  "I will be with you,
    because you need Me.
  I will be with them,
    because they need Me.
  I will help you and them,
    because you all need Me."

I will always have to
  live with bad people.
Help me, God, `
  so I won't follow them
    and do the bad things they do.

Psalm 13

Hey, God, how long are You
    going to forget me?
Forever?
How much longer will You
    hide up there by Yourself?
How much longer do I have to
    hurt like this?
How much longer will I want to
    cry all day long—
        and all night too?

Look at me, God!
Talk to me—now!

Don't let me be alone
    with people who hurt me.
I'm counting on You to help me, God.
I know You'll help me again.

Psalm 14

The dumb kids say,
  "There is no God."
They are the ones
  who say bad things
  and do bad things.

But I know there is a God
  and He watches us.
He is looking for kids
  to say *good* things
  and to do *good* things.

Even though we all do wrong things—
  me too—
God watches over us all.
And God asks:
  "Don't they know who I am?
  Don't they know that I know
    what they do?"

I guess they're scared of You, God.
That's why they say You aren't real.

But I know You will help us,
'cause Jesus is on our side.
We will be glad
  when we all know You.

Psalm 15

God:
>   Who can be Your friend?
>   Who can sit on Your lap?

I know who:
>   The ones who know
>   You help them do good things.
>   The ones who like
>   to hear what You say.
>   The ones who like
>   the people that You like.

God, You are my friend.
I am glad.

Psalm 16

Take good care of me, God,
    so I won't get hurt.
I tell You,
    "You are my God."
Thanks for the good things
    that You have given me.

Kids who don't know You
    don't know about
    all the good things You do.

I will tell them
    that You lead me where I should go,
    that You are always with me,
    that nothing can scare me.

You show me the way
    that leads to life.
Being with You makes me happy!

Psalm 17

Please listen, God!
    I want You to be fair.
I want to tell You how I feel.

I know You are on my side.
    You know me.
    You have looked at me.
    You have watched me.
    And You still love me.

I pray to You, God,
    because You listen to me
    and answer my prayers.
I know Your Son,
    and He said I could use His name
    as a reference when I talk to You.

I'm scared of some people.
I'm afraid when I think
    about some things.
But when I wake up every morning,
    I know You are with me.
That makes me happy.

Psalm 18

I love You so much, God!
> You watch over me.
> You take care of me.
> You hug me when I hurt.

When I have troubles,
> I ask You for help,
> and You help me.

Sometimes I think about dying.
> My mom, my dad—or I—might die.

Then I remember You, God,
> and they do too.

Even if they or I die,
> we will be with You.

Sometimes I think
> about car wrecks, robbers,
> or a fire that could burn our home.

We might have an earthquake
> or a war.

Sometimes I worry that
> my parents might get a divorce
> or they might lose their jobs
>> and we would be poor.

I worry about a lot of things, God.
But I also remember You.
You have always helped me before.
You will always help me, won't You?

29

Psalm 19a (vv. 1–6)

God,
when I look at the sky,
I can tell what You have been doing.
The sun, the moon, and the stars
    show that You keep things
    going all the time.
Every morning the sun shows us
    that You are still on the job.
Each night is Your promise
    for another day.
I don't need to hear Your voice.
I can hear what You are saying
    when I see what You do.

Psalm 19b (vv. 7–14)

Everything You say, God, is right.
You know what I should do
    and what I should not do.
You are fair in everything You do.
Whatever You decide is always right.
You're so smart that
    we can't even give You a grade.

I like Your rules,
    but I can't follow all of them.
I've probably done some wrong things
    that I don't even know about.
Just in case,
    forgive me for those things, too.
Please listen to the things I say
    and to the things I think.
You are the one who understands me.

Psalm 20

If you've got a problem,
    tell God about it.
He has helped me;
    He'll help you, too.

You can hear about Him at church.
    He'll listen to your prayers.
    He'll give you what is good for you.

Some kids think their parents
    will always take care of them.
Some think they can
    take care of themselves.
But I think we should
    let God take care of us.

You will hear us
    and help us,
    won't you, God?

Psalm 21

I watched the president today, Lord.
    He's always on TV.
    Everyone knows him.
    People always take his picture.
    What he says is important.

Look what You have given to him, God.
    He has a fancy house
        and bodyguards.
    He must be very rich.
    He never has to mow his yard
        or take out the garbage
        like my dad does.
    He will be in history books
        for my kids to read about.

But the president needs You, too.
    He needs someone to talk to and
        who won't tell reporters
        what he said.
    He needs someone to thank
        when things go great,
        or when nothing goes wrong.
    He needs to know that Jesus
        is his Savior,
        just as I do.

Thanks, God, for helping me.
Please help our president too.

Psalm 22—Echoes

My God, my God, why have
You abandoned me? (Ps. 22:1)
> *Jesus cried out with a loud shout, . . .*
> *"My God, My God,*
> > *why did You abandon Me?"* (Matt. 27:46)

All who see me make fun of me,
they stick out their tongues
    and shake their heads.
"You relied on the Lord," they say.
"Why doesn't He save you?
If the Lord likes you,
why doesn't He help you?" (Ps. 22:7–8)
> *Then they spat in His face and beat Him;*
> *and those who slapped Him said,*
> *"Prophesy for us, Messiah!*
> *Guess who hit You!"* (Matt. 26:67)
> *They spat on Him, and took the stick*
> *and hit Him over the head.* (Matt. 27:30)
> *[They] made fun of Him [and said,]*
> *"He saved others,*
> *but He cannot save Himself!"* (Matt. 27:41–42)

My throat is as dry as dust, and
my tongue sticks to the roof of my mouth. (Ps. 22:15)
> *[Jesus] said,*
> > *"I am thirsty."* (John 19:28)

They gamble for my clothes and
divide them among themselves. (Ps. 22:18)
> *[The soldiers] also took the robe,*

which was made of one piece of woven cloth
without any seams in it.
The soldiers said to one another,
"Let's not tear it;
Let's throw dice
  to see who will get it." (John 19:23–24)

All proud men will bow down to Him;
all mortal men will bow before Him. (Ps. 22:29)
  And so, in honor of the name of Jesus
  all beings in heaven, on earth,
  and in the world below
  will fall on their knees,
  and all will openly proclaim
  that Jesus Christ is Lord,
  to the glory of God the Father. (Phil. 2:10–11)

Psalm 23

When David was a boy he took care of sheep—and perhaps dreamed of being the king some day. When he became the king of Israel, he dreamed about the times when he was a boy taking care of the sheep.

David knew God had been good to him. He wanted to tell the people of Israel how God took care of them. So he talked to the people about God as a shepherd:

The Lord is my shepherd;
*   I have everything I need.*
He lets me rest in fields of green grass
*   and leads me to quiet pools of fresh water.*
He gives me new strength.
He guides me in the right paths,
*   as He has promised.*

Then an unusual thing happened. As David talked to the people about God, his mind wandered. He forgot that he was talking to the people, and he started talking to God:

Even if I go through the deepest darkness,
*   I will not be afraid, Lord,*
*   for You are with me.*
Your shepherd's rod and staff protect me.
You prepare a banquet for me,
*   where all my enemies can see me;*
You welcome me as an honored guest
*   and fill my cup to the brim.*
I know that Your goodness and love
*   will be with me all my life,*
and Your house will be my home
*   as long as I live.*

When David talked to God, he remembered how loving and kind God is. So he talked to the people about God.

When David talked to the people about God, he also remembered how loving and kind God is. So he talked to God.

Lord, when I talk to You,
    help me to remember others.
Lord, when I talk to others,
    help me to remember You.

Psalm 24

God, You've got it all!
You made the earth
    and the space it spins in.
You drew the plans.
You made the building blocks.
You put it all together.
It's all Yours!

Who can get an appointment to see You?
Who can drop by Your house for a visit?
Who can get Your unlisted number?
Only one who is perfect
    can get through to You.

But listen, God!
Pay attention!
You've got an appointment in Your book.
There's a knock at Your door.
Your phone is ringing.
Sit down in Your chair.
Open the door.
Answer the phone.
You've got company!

Who is this that can
    get through to You?
Who is this who
    is welcomed by You?

It is Jesus!
It is the one who came

from You to us
so He could die for our sins.

Now He comes
from us to You.
Now Jesus makes an appointment with You.
He knocks on Your door.
He rings Your bell.
And He brings us along!

Get ready, God!
You're going to have lots of company!

Psalm 25a (vv. 1–5)

I've got to talk to You, God,
    'cause I can't trust anyone else.

They call me a loser.
They laugh at me
    and point their fingers at me.
How can I be a loser
    when I trust in You?
How can they be winners
    when they say bad things about You?

Will You help me understand, Lord?
I can see how You run things,
    but I want to know why.
Why do You do things the way You do them?

I'm going to trust You,
    even though it doesn't make sense
    to me sometimes.

Psalm 25b (vv. 6–14)

Remember what kind of a God You are, Lord.
You are the one who got the idea
    to send Jesus to be a human with us.
You are the one who offered Him
    as the one to die to pay for our sins.

After You remember those things,
    then remember me.
When You remember what I've done wrong,
    remember Jesus died for me.
When you see the mistakes I make,
    see the Savior I have.

Then teach me, Lord.
I've learned *what* I should do
    and what I should not do.
Now would You teach me
    how to do what I should do
    and not to do what I should not do?
Learning the Ten Commandments
    hasn't been enough for me.
I still need Your help.
So let's start again, Friend.

Psalm 25c (vv. 15–22)

I've asked You for help, Lord,
     over and over again.
And I know You've helped me.
Here I am again.

Please listen with a kind ear,
     'cause I'm in the pits.
I'm scared.
I'm lonely.
I'm confused.
I've dug my way into lots of problems again.
Will You pull me out again?

Look at all the problems I have.
Look at all the things that could hurt me.
Please protect me.
I've got to trust You
     because I don't know anyone else
     who understands.

I know You've got a lot of other people, too,
     who depend on You.
Please help them also.

Psalm 26

Jesus, I want You to judge my case.
You are the only one who will find me "not guilty."

Look at me, Lord.
Listen to what I say.
Read my mind, not my lips.
Read my heart, not my actions.

You have let me in on Your secret.
When others judge me,
     when I judge myself,
     I am guilty.

But with You I am a different person.
You see me through the gift that You gave me.
In Your eyes, I am forgiven.
When You search me, You find Your grace,
     the gift You gave me.

That's why I like to worship You.
I want to hear Your Word;
     I want to receive You
     in the Supper You gave us.
I like to talk to You
     and listen to You.

When You are with me,
     I can be what You want me to be.

Psalm 27a (vv. 1–6)

Lord, You're the one
> who knows the way to go.
I'm not scared when You're
> the only one around.
But sometimes I am scared
> when I am with others.
Some kids offer me drugs at school.
>> They say I won't even have to pay.
>> They'll give them to me—
>>> the first time.
And I'm scared.

I thought Pat was one of my friends.
> But yesterday Pat showed me a magazine
> with dirty pictures.
> Pat wants to do something with me
>> that I don't want to do.
And I'm scared.

I ask You, Lord, for one thing—
> that is, one thing for today:
Please keep me close to You.
I want You to be with me.
I want You to guide me.
I want You to protect me.

Why should I do what others want me to do?
> Do they really want to help me?
If I follow them,
I will be like others who do those things.
And I don't like that.

I'd rather do what You want me to do.
　　　You care about me.
　　　You will help me be
　　　　　the kind of person You made me to be.

Psalm 27b (vv. 7–14)

Lord, listen to me when I talk to You.
I need an answer from You,
    and I need it now.

You invited me.
You said, "Come, worship Me."
I answered, "I will come, Lord."
So don't back out now.

Don't be mad at me,
    even though You have good reasons.
My parents are angry at me.
    They feel like giving up on me.
But, please, Lord, don't You give up.

Let me know what You want me to do, Lord.
    Make it real clear.
I admit I haven't done what You have told me to do,
    and I've done things You told me not to do.
But don't give up on me.

I know I can do better
    with Your help.
I trust You.
And I trust You to trust me.

Psalm 28

God, be my big brother!
    Be six feet tall.
    Look like You're on the football team.
    Don't shave for three days.
Then walk with me down the hall
    so no one will knock my books out of my hands.
Sit with me in the lunchroom,
    so others will want to be at my table.
Stand beside me
    when I have to give my report to the class.

Make them sorry that they have hurt me.
Show them the ways You have helped me.
Let them see what it's like
    to have You as a friend.

I want to praise You, Lord.
I want to let others know how great You are.
But You've got to do Your part.
I know how great You are.
You've got to learn to show off a little.

Shall we do it my way
    or Yours?

Psalm 29

God, You are the greatest!
    You've got it all!
    You've done it all!
    You are the greatest
    (to put it mildly)!

I can hear Your voice
    above all the voices in the lunchroom.
I can hear You speak
    among the roar at the game.
I can hear Your Word
    over the sounds of the band.

Your voice tells me You are with me.
I hear Your love
    by seeing what You do.
This world that You made
    is a great place to live.

God, You're the greatest!

Psalm 30

Thank You, God, for saving me—
    for saving me from me.
I thought everyone was laughing at me.
    Everything I did was wrong.
    I even wanted to laugh at myself,
        but it wasn't funny.

I wanted You to help, Lord.
I asked You to let me die.
But since You wouldn't do it,
    I decided to do it myself.

I thought about how I could do it—
    pills collected from my home and others;
    a leap from the overpass;
    the car running with the garage door closed.

Then I asked You to help again.
Thank You, God,
    for saying yes to my second prayer
    and not the first.
I will remember what You have done.
    My fear and anger were for only a night.
    Your love and patience are forever.
I may be scared at night,
    but You are there in the morning.

Now I feel safe and secure.
I used to feel worthless,
    and I wanted to die.
But I asked You:

"What do I gain by dying?
Can dead people enjoy life more
than unhappy living people?"
Dying like that is a waste,
a stupid waste.

You have changed my desire to die
into a desire to live.
You are my God,
the only one I've got.
I will thank You forever.

Psalm 31

I need Your help, God
Don't let me get hurt.
Hear me!
Save me now!
Be my bodyguard.
Don't let anyone hurt me.

They have set a trap for me.
They are using friendship as bait.
If I want to be one of the crowd,
    if I want to sit at their table,
    if I want to ride in their car,
I have to take the bait.

But it's a trap.
    A trap that will make me
        say things I don't want to say
    and do things that I
        don't want to do.
God, You can see what I want,
    and You can see what I will have to do
    to get it.
Help me, God; I'm in trouble.
I don't have to hide my tears from You.
I'm tired of crying.
I'm tired of feeling that I am alone.
They are all making fun of me.
Some of them point their fingers at me
    and call me names.
Worse yet, others don't even notice
    that I am here.

Will You help me, God?
Love me, and love me again even more.
Don't let me make a fool of myself.
Don't let me believe their lies.
Help me see what will happen
    if I walk into their trap.

Thank You, God, for listening.
You have helped me.
Now would You help them,
    and keep them off my back?

Psalm 32a (vv. 1–7)

What a relief!
I feel so clean, so new.
You have forgiven me, Lord!
You have taken me back into Your arms.
I can look at You again and smile.
Thank You, God.

When I refused to admit that I was wrong,
    I was miserable all the time.
I couldn't talk to You
    (except when I prayed before eating).
I felt dirty.
I was sad even when I laughed.

Then I said it.
I told You what You already knew.
I admitted what I had done.
The words I had to use were embarrassing,
    but I said them to You.
And You forgave me!

I was drowning in my sin
    until I climbed to the cross.
Others may understand my sins
    because they are guilty, too.
But You can forgive
    because You are not guilty,
    yet You died for me.
Thank You, Lord.

Psalm 32b (vv. 8–11)

God says:
>I will teach you.
>Will you learn?
>I know what is after tomorrow
>>and what is around the corner.
>
>Will you learn from Me?

>Don't be stupid
>>like a horse or a mule
>>that must be guided by
>>bridle and a bit in its mouth.

>Learn to think,
>>to make decisions,
>>to be responsible for yourself.

>I will teach you.
>>I love you
>>and want you to be with Me.

Psalm 33

Let's hear it for God!
Look at what He has done for us.
Let the music play!
Let's dance and sing!
We've got something to be happy about.

God is our friend.
He makes promises and keeps them.
He loves us so much that
    He wants to be with us.

The Lord made the earth,
    the faraway star
    and the close-up atom.
Everything we touch, see, hear,
    smell, and taste
    has been made by Him.
Praise the Lord!

The Lord looks down from heaven
    . to watch over us and protect us.
He sent Jesus to be here with us
    and to save us from ourselves.
He knows everything we do
    and everything we think.
And He still loves us.
Praise the Lord!

We don't have to depend on
    big armies or
    big bank accounts.

The Lord takes care of us.
We can trust in Him.
Praise the Lord!

Psalm 34

Come, my young friends, and listen to me,
and I will teach you to honor the Lord.
> Learn to thank the Lord.
> See and understand what He has done.
> Join with others in praising Him.

Come, my young friends, and listen to me,
and I will teach you to honor the Lord.
> Learn to pray to the Lord
> > when you need His help.
> He helps those who know
> > they are helpless.
> He sends His angels
> > to those in danger.

Come, my young friends, and listen to me,
and I will teach you to honor the Lord.
> Learn for yourself
> > how good God is.
> Rely on Him
> > to take care of you.
> Even the strong and the rich
> > don't have everything they want.
> Trust God to provide for you.

Come, my young friends, and listen to me,
and I will teach you to honor the Lord.
> Learn how to enjoy life
> > and how to be happy.
> Don't do the things that
> > hurt you and others.

Do the things and say the words
    that give peace and joy.

Come, my young friends, and listen to me,
and I will teach you to honor the Lord.
    Learn to listen to what
        God has to say.
    He wants to help you;
        He's on your side.
    Life may be confusing,
        but He's your guide.

Come, my young friends, and listen to me,
and I will teach you to honor the Lord.
    Learn that all suffering
        is not punishment from God.
    It's your way to grow,
        to understand others.
    Christ has suffered, too,
        so you need never hurt alone.

Come, my young friends, and listen to me,
and I will teach you to honor the Lord.

Psalm 35

I want my enemies to be Your enemies, Lord.
Let them be hurt in accidents.
Let them get sick.
Let them get an F in algebra.
Save me, Lord,
     by getting rid of them.

They have no reason not to like me.
They just think it's fun to pick on me.
They want to make themselves look good
     by making me look bad.

But I am not bad.
I may be different.
I may not dress like them
     or talk like them,
     but I am not bad.
I know You have created me, God.
And, Jesus, You are on my side.
I am not bad.

When I try to be nice to them,
     they ignore me.
When I do something good for them,
     they hurt me.
When they couldn't do their homework,
     I helped them.
I treated them like friends.
But when I got in trouble,
     they laughed at me.
They lied about me
     so other people wouldn't like me.

Isn't it time for You to help me, Lord?
I will give You credit.
I will go to church and thank You.

They are not my friends.
They tell bad things about me and
    point their fingers at me and say,
    "We saw what you did."
It's Your turn, Lord.
Wake up and show them who You are.
Make those who hurt me
    feel the pain they aim at me.

Lord, I just noticed something.
There are others who do like me.
They need friends,
    just as I do.
They would be glad to talk to me,
    to come to my house,
    to eat with me,
    to walk with me between classes.

Help me, Lord.
Help me see those who do like me,
    so I don't spend all my time
    thinking about those who hurt me.

Psalm 36a (vv. 1–4)

I can't see You today, God,
    because my sin has come between You and me.
My sin tells me that
    You can't hear me.
It says that You're not even there;
    and if You were there,
        You wouldn't care about me.
My sin tells me that this is the real me.
It tells me that if I want to get what I want,
    I should forget You
        and go for it.

I like me better when I'm with You
    than when I'm with my sin.
So that's why I'm talking to You.
I told my sin I was going to tell on it.
And I'm telling You.

Psalm 36b (vv. 5–12)

Jesus, I can see that Your love starts with me,
 but I can't see where it ends.
Your love is higher than the trees,
 the bank building,
 the mountains,
 the moon,
 the farthest star.
Is there no limit to Your love?

I can think about things that
 are close by and of everyday events—
  my teddy that I still keep (just in case),
  my family,
  my special place in the backyard,
  and other good things in life.
And I can think about things far away
 and beyond what I will ever see—
  an island in the South Pacific,
  a crater on the moon,
  a black hole in faraway space.
But Your love is both here and there—
 with the teddy
 and the black hole.

Thank You, Jesus,
 for being a part of my little world.
Thank You, Jesus,
 for letting me be a part of
  Your world beyond all worlds.

Psalm 37

"When you have to make a choice," they told me,
 "make two lists,
 so you can see what each choice offers."
Here are my two lists:

What Sin Offers

1. A lot of attention and everybody knows my name.
2. I can take from others, and I can get even.
3. Power to hurt those who are not as strong or as smart as I.
4. When good happens, I get the credit. When bad happens, I get the blame.
5. I make up my own mind and do what is best for me.
6. When I sin, I have to defend it—and repeat it.
7. I make a name for myself.

What God Offers

1. Peace with myself and long-range security.
2. Freedom from greed and the need for revenge.
3. The joy of helping those who need me.
4. When good happens, I thank You. When bad happens, I ask You for help.
5. You guide my decisions, and I do what is best for me and others.
6. When I sin, I admit it. You forgive me, and You help me do better.
7. You give me Your name.

Lord, You gave me the sense
 to make the lists.
Now give me the power
 to make the right choices.

Psalm 38

Please don't be mad at me, God!
I can feel Your anger.
Every time I take a step,
    I'm afraid I'll fall.
I'm afraid to answer the phone
    or open a letter
    because it might be bad news.

I know I was stupid.
I know I should not have done what I did.
I try to think of ways to punish myself.
I think that, if I hurt myself enough,
    I won't do such a stupid thing again.
I hurt, I tell You; I hurt!

You know what I want, don't You?
Please hear my groans—
    not just my silly words,
    but my screams.
My family pretends it didn't happen.
My friends won't talk to me about it.
But they think about it—
    and they talk about it
    when I'm not there.

But I trust You, God.
I know that I can't punish myself enough
    for what I did.
I know Jesus has already been punished for me.
He could take the punishment and survive.
I can't.

I confess my sin to You.
You have forgiven me.
Help me forgive myself.
Don't go away, God.
I need You like I've never
    needed You before.

Psalm 39

I thought I had solved my problem.
"I won't talk about it," I said to myself.
  "No one will know what I have done."

I was able to avoid talking about it,
  but I was not able to stop thinking about it.
Like a commercial on TV,
  the thoughts kept rushing through my mind.

While I was having a good time with friends,
  the thoughts would attack me.
When I was trying to study,
  the thoughts would take over.
In the middle of the night,
  the thoughts would be there.

How can I be freed from this?
It makes my life seem like a waste.
You're the only one I can trust, God.
Please listen to my thoughts.
Hear them as they are.
Forgive me, Lord.
And help me find someone
  that I can talk to.
Hear my prayer, Lord.
  Listen to my cry.
Share my life with me,
  so I can be happy.

Psalm 40a (vv. 1–5)

I waited for You to help me, Lord.
    I waited . . .
    and waited . . .

Then You did it!
You pulled me out of my depression.
You lifted me up
    and gave me joy.

I am glad that I can count on You
    to make me happy.
I don't have to pop pills
    or drink alcohol
    to be happy.

The happiness You give
    doesn't make me sick the next day.
Thanks for being my friend.

Psalm 40b (vv. 6-11)

Do I have to go to church today, Lord?
I know You've been good to me
    and all that.
I believe in You.
I pray to You.
Is that enough?

No, I don't have to go.
You won't love me any more—or less—
    just because I have perfect church attendance.
I don't have to go
    to impress You
    or anyone else.

But I can go to worship You
    because I want to.
You gave me ears to hear Your Word,
    and I'm going to use them.
You gave me friends who worship You,
    and I'm going to be with them.
You gave me friends who don't worship You,
    and I'm going to show them how it's done.

Lord, I know You'll always love me anyway.
That's why I want to worship You.

Psalm 41

You know I prayed for others
    when they were sick.
You heard my prayers, Lord,
    and You made those people well again.

Now I am sick.
I hurt.
For a little while,
    I didn't even want to live.

Those who come to see me do not help.
They say You are punishing me
    because I have sinned.
They say that if I really believed,
    You would make me well *right now*.
Some say I will never be well again.

But I don't care what they say.
I care what You say.
You say my sins are forgiven
    because Jesus is my Savior.
You say You will be with me
    even when I hurt and cry.
You say that I can even die,
    and I will live again.

That's good enough for me!

Psalm 42

Like a basketball team wants to win the play-off,
    I want to be with You, Lord.
I remember how I used to feel close to You.
    I knew all the answers.
    I sang the songs.
    I said the prayers.
    It seemed so easy.

But now I feel far away from You.
    I ask different questions,
        questions with no answers.
    I have new friends
        who have never heard of You.
    I'm doing what I want to do.
Why am I so sad?

I ask You one more time:
    Why have You forgotten me?
Don't You remember the fun we used to have?

Why am I so sad,
    and why do I have so many troubles?
Because I forgot You.

Please forget that I forgot.
I trust in You, God.
    You are my Savior and Friend.

Psalm 43

God,
tell them You have forgiven me.
Tell them I am innocent in Your eyes.
Since You have forgiven me,
    why should I feel guilty
    because of what they say?

Send out a search party to find me, Lord,
    and bring me back to You.
Then I will be happy again;
    then I will know I am with You.

Why am I so miserable?
Why do I care what others
    say about me?
As long as I trust in You,
    I know I'll be okay.

You're the only one who can save me,
    so keep me close to You.

Psalm 44

The Past

I've heard the story over and over again—
    at home,
    in Sunday school,
    in church,
    in confirmation class.
The story of Jesus:
    His birth in a barn—
        Mary and Joseph,
        angels and shepherds.
        "Oh, come, let us adore Him!"
    His life on earth—
        He healed the sick,
        He told the stories,
        He loved the strays.
        "Let us ever walk with Jesus."
    His suffering and death—
        betrayal and denial,
        nails and thorns,
        scorn and insults.
        "My God, My God, why have You abandoned Me?"
    His resurrection and ascension—
        an empty tomb and locked room,
        angels and women,
        now He's here, now He's not.
        Alleluia! Alleluia!
        "I know that my Redeemer lives."

The Present

Now is not like then.
You took Peter back.

Why not me?
You healed the woman who touched You.
　　What about Grandma?
If You died for us,
　　why did Mike die in a car wreck?
　　How could Lisa kill herself?
These aren't my questions, God.
Others ask me—and laugh at me.
　　"You go to church," they say.
　　"Tell us about your God.
　　Or is He too busy directing the angel choir?"
I want to hide.
I say dirty words to show
　　that I'm not religious either,
　　　　because I don't know the answers.

The Future
I still need You.
I have too many problems now.
To lose You would put me
　　over the edge.
I will still listen to You
　　and talk to You.
I will go to Your altar
　　to receive You in Communion.
I will sing the songs
　　and confess the faith.
I don't know the answers now,
　　but I know Your love.
　　　　"Jesus loves me, this I know."

Psalm 45

At a wedding. From the left side, fifth pew: a girl's view.
From the right side, sixth pew: a boy's view.

Left:
The groom looks so handsome standing there.
    Is it the tux?
    Or is it because he knows
        they are taking pictures of him?
Boys my age show off
    and try to act tough.
They think I should like them
    because they get attention.
Is he different?
Is he wonderful?
Or does he just look wonderful?

          Right:
          I wonder if I will ever do that.
          Could I look that good?
          Would a tux hide my awkwardness?
          Would it make me look sure and confident?
          What girl would want me, and only me,
               as long as she lived?

Left:
Look at her—
    she's beautiful!
Could I ever look like that?
Is it the dress or the hours
    she must have spent at the hairdresser?
She is so poised.

Would I cry or giggle if I were there?
What boy would ever want me
    to meet him at the altar?
Is there someone who acts silly now
    who will grow up to want me?
Will I be able to want one person
    for the rest of my life?

Right:
Wow! What a bride!
She's beautiful!
Girls I know will never look like that.
They giggle and pretend to like me;
        but when I try to show that I like them,
            they act like it's funny.
Is there a girl some place
    who will grow up and want me?

Center:
Some day we will walk down this aisle together.
We don't know each other now,
    but that's okay.
First, each of us needs to learn who we are alone,
    before we will be able to find
    someone we can share life with.
God, help me be a person
    who loves one other person for a lifetime.

Psalm 46

God is the one who protects us.
He is always with us,
> even when we are in big trouble.

We will not be afraid,
> even if our parents get a divorce,
> or if they lose their jobs,
> or if we have to move to another town.

Somewhere there is a place
> that is absolutely safe.

It is the place of God,
> and it is filled with joy.

God is in that place,
> and it will never be destroyed.

God, who created us, still claims us.
Jesus, who died for us, still lives with us.
We are not afraid.

Look at what God has done for us!
Wars are fought over and over again,
> and yet we survive.

Violence and sickness are everywhere,
> and yet we survive.

Hatred rages from generation to generation,
> and yet His love is here.

God, who created us, still claims us.
Jesus, who died for us, still lives.
We are not afraid.

Psalm 47

Let's hear it for God!
Three cheers for God!
He is great because He has power,
    and He uses His power with love.
He is great because He created everything,
    and He takes care of what He has made.
He is great because He knows how to be God.

God shows He is great
    by the power and wisdom of His creation
    and by sending His Son to be born in a barn.
God shows He is great
    in the splendor of nature and
    by giving His Son as a sacrifice on a cross.
God shows He is great
    by His great throne in heaven
    and His Son's empty grave on earth.

Let's hear it for God!
He's the greatest!

Psalm 48

When I am in church,
    it seems so simple.
God is in charge of us
    and in love with us.
We are safe and secure.
    We are together.

But at school,
    God is a joke.
His name is used to hate
    instead of to love.
I have to pretend
    that I am cool.
I have to hide tears
    and hurts and fears.
I have to laugh at the
    new ones, the weak ones.
I have to be like those
    who are not like me.

But with You, God,
    I can be weak,
    and I can like those
        who are also weak.
    I can cry or laugh.
    I can be me.
Only then am I safe enough
    to love myself as I am
        and others as they are.

Psalm 49

Listen up, everyone!
Pay attention!
I've got it all figured out,
    and I want to tell you
        before I lose it again.

I feel good about me.
    I am not afraid.
It's not because I am so good,
    and certainly not because
        I am better than others.
We can't make ourselves feel good about ourselves.
We can't put down others to lift ourselves up.
We can't make our own lives worthwhile.

But Jesus has done it for us.
    We don't have to deserve it.
    He gave Himself to be our Savior.
    We are worthwhile only because
        His death and resurrection
        make us worthwhile.

We don't have to make lots of money
    to prove how important we are.
Look what happens to rich people.
    They get sick and die
    just like everyone else.

We don't have to become famous
    so everyone will know our name.
We don't have to have our pictures

on TV or in the papers.
Famous people get sick and die
    just like everyone else.

The best way to learn how to live
    is to learn how to die.
    Get it over with! Out of the way!
And Jesus did that for us.
He didn't just teach us how to die.
He didn't just show us the way to do it.
    He *did* it—
    and He did it *for us*.
Now we can live without fearing death.

Those who believe in Jesus will die
    just like everyone else.
But we will live again with Him.

Psalm 50

Now hear this:
    God has something to say.
    Get together and pay attention!

God says:
"You are My people
    because I created you,
    because I saved you,
    because I called you,
    because I want you
        to be with Me.

"I do not need you to defend Me.
    You do not make My Word true.
    You do not make My church grow.
    Your love does not save the world.

"I am not scolding you
    for teaching My Word,
    working for My church,
    and loving My people.
I let you do those things
    because you are My people,
    and I want you to share My joy.
So don't work for Me
    as though I need to depend on you.

"You are not doing Me a favor
    when you wear a cross,
    when you go to youth events,
    when you sing My praise.

81

"If you want to serve Me,
      recognize what I have done for you,
      and give Me the credit.
And when you need help,
      ask Me for it.
      I will help you.
      Then you'll learn
            how to worship Me.

"Don't think that
      you can make up for the wrong things you do
      by trying to do an equal amount
            of good for Me.
I have already forgiven you.
My Son paid for your sins long ago.

"I'm glad when you believe in Him
      and when you love Him
      and want to serve Him.
But serve Me because you are free,
      not because you feel guilty
      or because you want a favor from Me.

"Listen to what I have to say.
Don't try to tell Me how to do My job.
Do it with Me!"

Psalm 51

Lord, have mercy!
Because Your love has no limits!
Christ, have mercy!
Wipe away my sins!
Lord, have mercy!
And make me clean!

I'll admit that I do wrong things.
I can't forget my sins.
I have sinned against You, God,
only against You.
I have done what You told me
not to do.
You would be right if
You sent me to hell.
Sin is a part of who I am.
It has been since I became me.

Lord, have mercy!
Because Your love has no limits!
Christ, have mercy!
Wipe away my sins!
Lord, have mercy!
And make me clean!

Lord, You want me to be honest with You.
Fill my mind with Your wisdom.
If You take away my sins,
then I will be forgiven.
If You wash me,
then I will be clean.

I want to laugh and sing again.
    I want to feel free and alive.
Erase all my sin.
Flush away all my evil.

Lord, have mercy!
    Because Your love has no limits!
Christ, have mercy!
    Wipe away my sins!
Lord, have mercy!
    And make me clean!

Transplant a pure heart into me, O God.
    You be the donor.
Give me a new and faithful attitude.
Don't send me away from You.
Don't take Your Holy Spirit from me.
Fill me with the joy of knowing
    that You have saved me.
Then I will tell other sinners
    what You will do for them.

Lord, have mercy!
    Because Your love has no limits!
Christ, have mercy!
    Wipe away my sins!
Lord, have mercy!
    And make me clean!

Let me live a long life, Lord,
    and let me live it for You.
Give me the ability to tell
    Your Good News to others.

You don't want me to show off
    so others will see how good I am.
You want me to be humble
    and know that I depend on You.

Lord, have mercy!
    Because Your love has no limits!
Christ, have mercy!
    Wipe away my sins!
Lord, have mercy!
    And make me clean!

Psalm 52

I can't understand you people!
You brag about the things
    you should be ashamed of.

One is proud of the fact
    that he has had sex with seven girls.
Another's claim to fame
    is the ability to drink six beers a night.
Some think they are great because they steal,
    others because they cheat at school.
They lie—and are proud of it!
They hate—and think it makes them important!

Don't you know you are hurting yourselves?
People may want to have sex with you,
    but they won't want to love you
        and stay with you.
Some people may think you're big stuff,
    but they won't trust you.
You may hold your booze now,
    but how long before it has a hold on you?

People who know what is right
    will not admire you.
They will understand that
    you are tying to make a name for yourself.
But they depend on God.
    They take the name He gave them:
        "Christian."

God, I am not better than others.
    I know that.
But I am glad that the goodness
    I have comes from You.
As a rose bush blooms when it is watered,
    I grow when You cover me with Your love.
I will always thank You, God,
    for what You have done.
And I want others to know
    that I depend on You.

Psalm 53

I caught You, God!
You gave us this one before—
    Psalm 14 is the same thing.
Did You forget and repeat Yourself?
Or are You checking us out
    to see if we pay attention?

But I read it again
    since You said it again.
Maybe there's a message
    in Your double message.

A fool says, "There is no God."
And he says it again: "There is no God."
And again!
And again!

The fool who says there is no God
    does not make You disappear.
My saying "There *is* a God"
    does not make You appear.
You are what You are.
You are love—
    so You became a human
    so we could see You and know You.

I heard Your word that created.
I heard Your word from a mountain.
I heard Your word from a scroll.
And then You became the Word in a human.

Yet sometimes we still don't hear You,
      even when we see You.
So we have to be told again . . .
      and again.
And the fool will still ask,
      "Who's that?"

Psalm 54

Think of the power You have, God.
    It can't be measured.
    It can't be compared to other powers.
    It can't be used up.
Use that power—all of it—
    to help me, Lord.
Listen to my prayer—please.

Look what others are trying to do to me.
They are trying to hurt me.
They make me feel bad about myself.
They don't care about me—or You.

But You are my helper, God.
The evil they say about me
    will hurt them, not me.

I am glad I can worship You, Lord.
    I give You thanks
        because You are good.
You are with me when I need You.
You are always beside me.

Psalm 55

Listen!
Don't put me on hold!
Don't hang up on me, Lord!
I need Your help.

Bad thoughts come to my mind.
I wonder if I could die.
I wonder if I could take pills
    and fly away from my problems
        like a bird flying toward the clouds
           to escape the problems on the ground.
I wonder if drinking beer or hard stuff
    would free me from this pain.
I need some place to hide from me.

I can take it when my enemies hurt me.
You have answered my prayers for help.
But now my best friend
    has turned against me.
My friend, who shared my secrets,
    who went to church with me!
Now my friend shares my secrets with others.
Now my friend laughs at me
    because I worship You.

I gripe and complain—
    and You hear me
        as though You think I am praying.
You keep promises You haven't even made.
Yet my best friend broke the promises
    that he/she made to me.

He/she talks a good line
    with words that are full of pity,
    but there is hatred in his/her heart.

I can trust only You, Lord,
    the one friend who will not
        turn away from me.
Help me be a friend to others.

Psalm 56

Have mercy on me, God.
Pay attention to me!
Look at my enemies who want to hurt me.
Look at those who mess up my life.
I am afraid, God.
I know that You,
    and You alone, can help me.
What can my enemies do to me
    if You are on my side?

My enemies have names.
Help me name them.

My enemy is Fear:
    Fear that I can't be what I want to be.
    Fear that I will be what I don't want to be.
    Fear that I can't stay in control.
    Fear that I will lose what I have.
    Fear that I will kill myself,
        or get AIDS, or be a dope-head.

My enemy is Failure:
    Have You kept a record of my failures?
    Will I keep on making the same mistakes?
    Am I a failure in my family?
    Will I go to hell?

My enemy is The Unknown:
    What will happen to me?
    Will I make the same mistakes
        my parents make?

Will pollution or war
　　　or violence or drugs ruin
　　　the world that I will live in?

I have enemies, Lord.
　　　I have Proper Paranoia.
But I also have You.
I am afraid when I am alone,
　　　but not when I know I am with You.
I can fail but not be destroyed
　　　because You are with me.
I don't have to be sure of myself
　　　because I am sure of You.

Psalm 57

Remember that You love me, God!
I see the world from two points of view.
I need Your help to know which is true.

When I sit on Your lap,
    I can look and see
        and not be afraid.
I can see my sin and not feel guilty
    because I know You have forgiven me.
I can see how others have hurt me
    and not be angry
    or try to get even
    because You have forgiven them, too.
I can see sickness, accidents, even death
    and not be afraid.
I know that Jesus was a survivor—
    even of death—
    and I will be, too.

But I have another view,
and it is also true.

When I jump from Your lap
    to the garbage pit of life,
    my sin becomes a big secret
    that hides in my gut
    and haunts my sleep.
Then I see the power that others have—
    power to hurt me,
    power to make me not like myself,
    power to make me deny You.

And I see the power I have—
    power to make others not like themselves,
    power to laugh at others,
    power to say and do evil.
And I see the dangers of the world—
    danger of ruining my whole life
        by one stupid choice,
    danger of destroying myself
        and my family,
    danger of wasting the one life I have.

Both views are true.

I need You, Lord.
Get my attention.
Dazzle me with Your glory.
Splash Your love all over the place.
Let me be so amazed by You
    that I never look at the other view.

Psalm 58

It's not fair, God!
It's not fair.

Parents are supposed to be fair,
	aren't they?
But they're not.
And teachers aren't either.

And You're not always fair either, God.
You've helped others
	when You didn't help me.
You've given things to others
	that I don't have.

What if everything were fair?
	We'd all be exactly alike.
I don't know if I'd like that.
If everything were fair,
	we'd all be punished for our sin.
I know I wouldn't like that.

Maybe You don't know how to be fair, God.
But I am glad that
	You know how to forgive us
	and how to make each of us special
	in our own way.
Teach me Your way.

Psalm 59

Save me from my enemies, God:
    from those who drink and drive,
    from those who play with guns,
    from those who would give me AIDS.

I could be killed in many ways.
    I know it has happened to others.
I don't have to be the one who's dumb
    to be the one who dies.
Those who do stupid things
    take others with them,
    even when they die.

Protect me, Lord God Almighty.
    Don't let me think
        like those who cause death.
    Don't let me follow the crowd
        over the edge.
    Don't let me think I have to risk my life
        just to show I'm cool.

Some kids want to live
    like they're on a violent TV show.
But they don't have a stunt man
    to take their place in a fall.
But I've got You, Lord.
    You are my friend.
    You love and protect me.
Teach me to follow Your way.

Psalm 60

Why have You turned against me, God?
Don't You like me any more?

Our team loses again and again.
My grades are going down.
My friends don't call
    as often as they used to.
My parents are so busy
    they never talk to me.
What's going on, God?

And God answers:
"I have not forgotten you.
I must let you fail
    so you will appreciate success.
I must let you be alone
    so you learn to love yourself—
    and then you can let others love you.
I must let others
    be less than perfect
        in the way they treat you
    so you learn that you need
        to do your part in a relationship."

Okay, God, I hear You.
    You haven't rejected me;
    You've just been loving me
        in strange ways.
With You as my friend, I can't lose.

Psalm 61

Listen to my problems, Lord,
    problems I never thought I'd have.
For years I have wanted to be away from home,
    away from family,
    away from classmates,
    away from relatives,
    away from church.

And now it's happened!
I'm away.
        No family!
        No classmates!
        No relatives!
        No church!
        No one!

Will You still be with me?
Can I still come to worship You?
Can I find a place to feel at home with You
    when I am far from where we used to meet?

Thanks for being with me here, Lord.
Please stay with me wherever I go,
    and I'll always look for You.

Psalm 62

Do You know how much time I spend waiting, Lord?
I wait for the school bus.
I wait for teachers who are late for class.
I wait for parents more than they wait for me.
I wait in line all the time.
And I have to wait for You, too, Lord.

Why are You so slow in answering my prayers?
Why does it take so long to get through to You?
I know about world population
    and that other people have more problems than I do.
But that's not supposed to make any difference.
Do I have to take a number to talk to You?
Couldn't You get "call waiting"?

But I have to wait on You
    because I have no choice.
You don't have any competition.
There's no one else I can ask for help.
You, and You alone, hear my prayers.
You are the one who has saved me from sin and death.
You know the past and hold the future in Your hands.
I have to wait for You.
No one else will do.

Psalm 63

Lord, You are on my mind all the time.
I am the sponge;
    You are the water.
Without You, I am dry and rough.
    With You, I am fresh and soft.

I like to hear Your Word
    and be with You in Holy Communion.
I like to thank and praise You.
You give meaning to my life.

As I go to bed, I remember You.
You have gotten me through the day.
You forgive my sin.
You help me see a happy world.
I feel You tuck me into bed
    like my mother used to do.

I know I have problems,
    and I know I make most of them for myself.
But as long as I am with You,
    I am safe and secure.

Psalm 64

Hey, God, I need You!
You are my 911, my call for help.
I'm all alone.
I had friends last week;
    this week they are my enemies.

Last week we laughed together;
    this week they laugh at me.
Last week we talked together at school
    and on the phone;
    this week they talk about me.
Last week I told them my secrets;
    this week they tell everyone my secrets.

Come and be with me, Lord,
    because I am alone.
No—go be with them.
Get into their hearts
    and change them.
Love them
    so they can love me again.

Psalm 65a (vv. 1–4)

In the name of the Father
    and of the Son
    and of the Holy Spirit.
    Amen.

Here I am in church again.
I am keeping the promises that I made.
I'm here to hear Your Word,
    to receive You in Your Supper,
    to worship You and to serve You.

And You are keeping Your promises, too.
You are here with me.
You have forgiven my sins.
You are hearing my prayers.

We've got to go on meeting like this.

Psalm 65b (vv. 5–13)

We have come to worship You, Almighty God,
    to thank You for all that You have done for us.

You have given us more than we can use
    and yet made us responsible for the way we use it.
You have blessed us with food,
    yet some are hungry because we don't share.
You have blessed us with beautiful homes,
    yet some are homeless unless we invite them in.
You have blessed us with beauty and resources in nature,
    yet we have made some things ugly
        and wasted others.
You have blessed us with the freedom to worship You,
    yet many won't unless we tell them about You.

When we say thank you among ourselves,
    we reply, "You're welcome."
When we say thank You to You,
    You say, "Share it."

I think You know us
    better than we know ourselves.

Psalm 66

Two! Four! Six! Eight!
Jesus, You are really Great!

You're the only one who uses love
    to change the world.
You're the only one who gave His life
    to save all people.
You're the only one
    who forgives our sins
    and cures our death
        by giving us life again.

Two! Four! Six! Eight!
Jesus, You are really Great!

You have helped us
    but do not control us.
You have paid for us
    then set us free.
You have chosen us
    but have not forced us to choose You.

Two! Four! Six! Eight!
Jesus, You are really Great!

I will serve You
    because I am free not to.
I will hear Your Word
    because I want to know
    what You've got to say.
I will love those whom You love,
    just as You love me.

Two! Four! Six! Eight!
Jesus, You are really Great!

Psalm 67

God, bless our family,
    and keep us close to You.
Help us to share with one another
    the love You have given to us.

May our family praise You, O God;
    may all the people praise You.

God, bless all my friends,
    and keep us close to You.
Help us to share with one another
    the love You have given to us.

May all my friends praise You, O God;
    may all the people praise You.

God, bless our nation,
    and keep us close to You.
Help us to share with one another
    the blessings You have given to us.

May all the nations praise You, O God;
    may all the people praise You.

Psalm 68

God, look at Your record in history.
You always win.
Hitler thought he had You beat.
Communism thought it had replaced You.
They won some battles,
    but You won the war.

Some who have money and power,
    some who lead armies
        and control business
    think they don't need You.
Because they don't need You,
    they want You out of the way.
They fight against You.

But the poor people,
    the sick, the homeless,
    those who see their own sin
        instead of looking for the sin of others,
    the lonely, the afraid—
    they all need You.
Because they need You,
    some love You and serve You.

Look how You have led Your people.
You did not come with power to scare them
    or with gifts to bribe them.
But You came as one of us,
    a baby,
    in a family,
    in a community,

in a school,
in a nation.
Like us.

You gave Your perfect life
     for our messed up lives.
Because You died for us,
     we can now live for You.
People who knew You
     loved You so much
     that they told others.
Those who heard them
     loved You so much
     that they told others.
(But why did some who heard the message
     hear it only for themselves
     and feel no need to tell others?)
The Good News jumped from Palestine
     to Africa, to Europe,
     to the Americas,
     around the world and back again.

Praise the Lord,
     who helps us every day.
He is the God who saves us.
He is our God,
     who gives us life now and forever.

We don't have to be afraid
     when we see His enemies win battles now.
Strong people will still depend on their own strength.
Worldly wise people will still depend on their own wisdom.
Rich people will still depend on their money.
But we will depend on the grace of God.

110

Show us how You have won in the past, Lord!
Remind us that You won by dying,
    not by killing.
Let us see the victories You won
    by giving rather than by taking.

I haven't yet figured out what life means, Lord.
And I don't think many adults have either,
    not even those who pretend they know.
But You know about life, Lord.
You have it figured out.
So I'll just go along with You.

Psalm 69

Prologue
Save me, Lord!
I'm in hot water up to my neck.
I'm swimming upstream.
The waves are lapping over me,
    and I'm about to drown.
I've called for help,
    but no one listens.
I have looked to You for rescue,
    but You are not here.

Act 1
There are a lot of people
    who could get me into trouble.
My sister could tell my parents.
My friend could tell the secrets
    that we have shared.
You, Lord, are the only one
    who knows everything about me.
You are the only one who knows me
    and loves me anyway.
I am glad I don't have any secrets from You.
I never had to worry
    what You would think about me
        if You found out
    because You already know.

Act 2
I cannot live in fear that
    others will tell on me.
I ask You to help me, God.

112

Help me in the time and the way
    that You choose.
Don't let others throw mud at me.
Don't let me be destroyed
    by the flood of fear
        that comes over me.

Act 3

You know what I want, Lord.
Get those who are out to get me!
Beat them to the punch.
Ruin their reputations
    before they ruin mine.
Look up their names in Your records
    and see their mistakes.
Tell everyone about them.
Make others laugh at them.

Act 4

But I hurt all the more
    when I ask You to hurt them.
Do not treat them like they treat me.
Instead, treat them like You treat me.
Let them also learn of Your love.
You listen to me when I need You;
    please listen to them also.
Then You can help us together.
Just as our faults have divided us,
    so Your love can bring us together.

Psalm 70

I thought they were my friends, Lord.
They invited me to be with them.
We talked on the phone.
But now they want me to do things
    that would hurt me.

I know that smoking pot will hurt me.
    But they want me to do it.
I know that popping pills could kill me.
    But they want me to do it.
I know that if I did the sex things they talk about,
    I would hurt me,
        and someone else.
Unless I do what they want me to do,
    I can't be their friend.

Lord,
    I want Your friends to be my friends,
    and my friends to be Your friends.
I am weak and afraid.
I need people to like me.
But I also have to like myself.
Be my friend, God.
I need You!

Psalm 71

Lord, my grandparents are old.
I didn't know that
    until they came to visit this time.
I hadn't noticed that they walk funny,
    that their skin is dry and wrinkled,
    that they don't hear what I say.

What will I be like when I am old?
You have always been a part of my life.
I don't even remember a time
    when I didn't know You.
Will it always be that way, Lord?
I know I will grow up.
    I won't depend on my parents to support me.
    I won't always be in school,
        with others teaching me.
    I won't always need someone to tell me
        to eat the right foods,
        to go to church,
        to clean my room
        and brush my teeth.

But can I still be Your kid,
    even when I am old?
Can I still depend on You
    to take care of me?
Can I still count on You
    to be the one who understands?

Yes, God! Yes!

I will always depend on You.
You will always be my God.
I will always need You.
I will cry to You for help.
And I will praise You.

Psalm 72

Today, Lord, we studied about government.
I learned how everything is supposed to work.
But what I learned in class
    is not what I see on TV.

I learned that we are the government,
    because we vote to elect our leaders.
    But I know lots of people who don't vote.
I learned that we pay our taxes
    to provide education, safety, justice.
    But I know money is wasted and stolen.
I learned that our leaders are public servants,
    selected and elected to help all people.
    But I see how they serve those who reelect them.
    I see how they use their jobs for their gain.
    I see that they do not tell the truth.

At first, I wanted to give up.
Why should I ever vote?
Why should I pay taxes?
Why should I run for office
    or work for the government?

That's why I came to talk to You about it, Lord.
If I must ask the questions,
    I must also listen to Your answers.

You have taught me what I should be;
    yet I have done what I should not do
    and not done what I should do.
But You have not given up on me.

You still love me.
You sent Jesus to be my Savior.
I am forgiven.
I'm glad that I can know both what I should be
and also that I am loved,
even when I fail.

Just as I see my sin,
so I can see the wrongs of my government.
It is a better government because
it does not hide its wrongs—
at least it doesn't always get away with things
when it tries to cover up.
Our government has survived—
not because it is perfect,
but because it cannot always
hide its imperfection.
We can survive even the bad leaders
because they must face those who vote.

Lord, thank You for the government we have.
Help us to make it better.
Give Your blessings and guidance to
the president and every governor,
the men and women of Congress,
the judges and those who enforce the laws,
the members of the president's cabinet,
those who work in offices,
those who do the little jobs.

Bless other governments, too, Lord.
Help our nation 'be a part of a peaceful world.

We praise You, Lord God,
the Creator of all the world
    and all the people in it.
May all the people of the world know You.
May Your name be holy everywhere.

Amen! Amen!

Psalm 73

God, I know they say You are good,
    and sometimes I agree.
But there are times when I can't see it.
Sometimes I think that You don't care
    or can't help.
It doesn't make sense to me
    when I see people who do bad things
    getting all the good things out of life.

Those who ignore You,
    laugh at You,
        and break all Your laws
    are strong and healthy.
They've got money.
They get good grades.
They brag about everything they do—
    not only the good things but
    also the things I'd be ashamed of.
They cheat in school,
    steal from stores,
    say awful things about parents and teachers.
And even good people listen to them
    and want to be their friends.
They say, "God doesn't know what we do.
    He's busy with the big issues of the world.
    He won't know what we do."
Am I stupid because I'm still a virgin,
    because I work for my money,
    because I don't do drugs,
    because cigarette smoke makes me sick?
God, it seems to me that I get punished

for doing good.
I need help from You, God.
I am talking to You because
  You know me better than anyone else
  and You love me more than anyone else.
I know that the bad things they do cause sorrow—
  sorrow for their parents and others now,
  sorrow for themselves in the future.
I know someday they will wish
  they had not done those things.

When I get jealous of others,
  I become a bitter person.
  I lose the joy of living.
But when I talk to You,
  I see things in a different way.
I am not doing You a favor
  when I do what You tell me to do.
You are doing me the favor
  when You help me do what You tell me to do.
When I do wrong, You forgive me
  because Jesus has been punished in my place.
But that's not all!
The same love from Jesus that forgives sin
  also helps me avoid sin.
I am weak, God,
  so weak that I must depend on You for everything.
Don't let me think that I am better than others.
Help me share Your love with others.

Psalm 74

Why don't You take better care
    of Your church, God?
You gave us Your Son as our Savior.
You called us to be Your people.
You could give us everything else, too.
You could make us rich.
You could give us power.
You could make other people see
    that You have made our hearts different.
But You don't.

People laugh at the church
    and say it is out of date.
The church never has enough money.
The members argue with each other.
Newscasts show church leaders
    who do bad things.

They laugh at You, too, God.
They judge You by the kind of people
    who claim to belong to You.
How long are You going to put up with it?
When will You do something?

Jesus said He came for the sinners and outcasts.
He was always looking for the lost sheep.
I guess He got what He wanted;
He got us.
He suffered and died for people like us.
And the church will continue to suffer and die
    if it still reaches the sinners and outcasts,

if it still goes searching for lost sheep.
Is that Your message, Lord?
Do we have to see
    and to show
    our failures
    so we remember we live on Your love?

Help us, Lord.
Help us be humble.
Help us look for mercy,
    not honor and success.

Psalm 75

Thank You, God;
 thank You once for being You,
 and thank You again for the things You do.

"Some day I will come to judge you,"
 Jesus said.
"I will be fair when I judge you,
 but some will be afraid.
Trust Me!
Don't be scared of My judgment;
 I will not judge what you have done,
 but what I have done for you.
Think about it:
 You don't have to hide the bad things you've done.
 You don't have to brag about the good things.
I will judge you by the life I lived for you.
Trust Me on this one."

I hear You, Jesus.
If I could pick my judge, it would not be
 one of my teachers or a cop
 or one of my friends,
 not even my mother.
I want You to be my judge, Jesus.
I know that the ones who want to judge themselves
 end up proving they are guilty.
 The more they try to prove they are right,
  the more wrong they are.

But You judge me by Your grace.
>   You give me what You want me to have
>   instead of what I deserve.
I like that, Jesus.
I like to talk about You.
When I know You are around,
>   life makes more sense.

Index by Psalm